Easy-to-Make Books That Target Specific Reading Needs

Templates, Easy How-to's, and Lessons That Support Each
Child With Books Matched to Individual Reading Needs

Florence Miyamoto
and Joan Novelli

New York • Toronto • London • Auckland • Sydney
Mexico City • New Delhi • Hong Kong • Buenos Aires

Teaching
Resources

To my husband, Olen and my sons,
Max, Chris, and Jason

—F.M.

"Just as a listener tunes in to a speaker, so a teacher must observe, listen to, and tune in to a learner."

—Marie M. Clay, *By Different Paths to Common Outcomes* (Stenhouse, 1998)

Editor: Joan Novelli
Cover design by Jason Robinson
Interior design by Holly Grundon
Interior illustrations by James Graham Hale and Maxie Chambliss

ISBN-13: 978-0-439-43829-2
ISBN-10: 0-439-43829-2

Contents

Easy-to-Make Books

About This Book

Anail points to the capital *A* in her name and in her friend Ana's name. "You have one like mine," she says. Anail's not quite sure what the letter *A* is. She only knows it belongs to her and she knows how to draw it.

This interest in letters comes naturally to children, who have a strong desire to learn how to make sense of those squiggles and lines so they can be readers. However, it is very difficult to find a simple readable text for a child who has limited word knowledge. This includes children in any classroom who are at the beginning stages of learning to read, children who are experiencing challenges around reading, and English language learners who are learning to read while also acquiring a new language.

What do you do? You write books just for them. Books with children's names, books featuring their pets and favorite places, books about their birthdays . . . these are just a few of the simple books you can make using the lessons and reproducible templates in this book. In *The New Kindergarten: Teaching Reading, Writing & More*, author Connie Leuenberger writes: "The desire to read is key to reading success. We must make children burn to read stories on their own. We need to fill their days with literature that they can relate to and that makes them want to pick up books again and again" (2003, p. 89). These easy-to-make books, created especially for the children reading them, will nurture that desire to read and keep children coming back as they gain knowledge of concepts about print, build word recognition skills, develop comprehension strategies, and experience the rewards as learners that lead to reading success.

Before You Begin

Assessment guides instruction, and when it comes to teaching reading, assessment is the starting point. Close analyses of observations gathered during daily lessons are the tools that help teachers learn more about each child. From these observations, ideas for books will naturally emerge. For example, consider the observations of Anail as she

works to make sense of the letter she finds at the beginning of her name. A "letter book" made just for her will start Anail on the way to learning more about her special letter. Simple pages featuring the letter *A* and pictures whose names, like Anail's, begin with *A* will help her acquire important alphabet recognition skills. From there, Anail's collection of letter books may grow to include a book for every letter. As her knowledge grows, Anail will be taking an important step in learning to read—being able to name and recognize letters. (For more on Letter Books, see page 21.)

When creating books for children, Marie Clay, in *Literacy Lessons Designed for Individuals, Part One* (2005a), suggests starting with the following.

* a very easy storybook

* a very simple story you have read to the child

* a simple book about an experience the child has had

* a simple story that you write for the child, keeping to the child's known vocabulary

* a simple text the child dictates

Notice the key words here: *child*, *easy*, and *simple*. Write with a certain child in mind, using the child's own vocabulary. Ask yourself, "What will make this easy for this child?" Keep the following considerations in mind, based on guidelines provided in *Bridges to Literacy: Learning From Reading Recovery* (DeFord, Lyons, & Pinnell, 1991).

* consistent layout of the print

* strong picture support

* simple language structures

* memorable, repetitive language patterns

* use of known letters or words

* meaningful content

* short in length

Important Objectives

One of the most important objectives is to establish and secure the early behaviors of reading. These are observable behaviors that a child must have under control to become a reader. The chart on page 6 summarizes these behaviors and suggests how to create books that support children in developing these skills. In addition to the following teacher and student objectives for establishing the behaviors of a reader, continue to ask yourself, and answer, in innovative ways, these questions: What will I, as the teacher, need to do to help the child achieve reading success? What will the child need to do to achieve reading success?

Objectives for the Teacher

* To become a better observer

* To teach within the child's "zone of proximal development" (see right)

* To model what good readers do

* To honor approximations

* To create a safe learning environment

Teaching Tip

The zone of proximal development (ZPD), a concept developed by psychologist Lev Vygotsky, refers to the levels at which the development of a behavior occurs: "The lower level is the child's independent performance, what the child knows and can do alone. The higher level is the maximum the child can reach with help and is called assisted performance" (Bodrova & Leong, 1996).

Objectives for the Child

❋ To help the child see herself or himself as a reader

❋ To help the child attend to print

❋ To help the child become actively engaged in learning

❋ To establish and secure the early behaviors of reading

❋ To know and practice the early concepts about print (see chart below)

❋ To develop strategic reading behaviors, such as rereading, self-correcting, and searching for meaning cues using pictures, the story, and the word

Early Reading Behaviors

If the Child Needs Support With . . .	Create Books With These Features . . .
One-to-one matching	• Exaggerate the spaces between words. (See Long Books, page 65.) • Place small dots beneath each word and have the child touch the dots as he or she reads. I like cats.
Left-to-right directional movement	• Place a green dot at the beginning of the line of print. • Use only one line of text on a page. • Write the text in a consistent place across the top of each page.
Known words	• Write books using the child's name. • Write books using known letters (and their sounds) and words.
Unknown words	• Write books using a predictable pattern. • Use repetitive language.
Searching (looking for meaning cues in letters, words, and pictures)	• Make pop-up books to encourage the child to stop and look at the picture for meaning cues. • Change the pattern on the last page of the books, still keeping to known words, to encourage the child to stop and look at known letters and words.

Getting Started

The lessons and personalized books in this collection can be used in any order that best supports the needs of your students. As you review them, think about the specific needs in your classroom and consider creating a list to match books to children. You might, for example, have several children with little letter knowledge who would benefit from alphabet books that use pictures to link letter shapes and names. The Letter Books (page 21) will be just right for these students. For children who are discovering that letters come together to form words, the Name Books (page 47) are a great place to start. And for students who are ready to put words together to build sentences, the Long Books (page 65) let them assemble sentences based on their own words and interactive writing. With dozens of books to choose from, you will have books to meet the needs of all your students as they grow and learn.

Continue to watch for change over time. As children take on new learning, you will want to make adjustments to the new books you write for them, such as changes in the layout of the print, predictable patterns, and known letters and words. The following chart suggests scaffolding techniques for making these sorts of modifications so that you can continue to support children in growing as readers.

Scaffolding Strategies

Features of Books	Scaffolding Strategies
Predictable Patterns	• Begin with a predictable pattern. • Change the pattern on the last page of the book, still keeping to the child's known words.
Print Layout	• Begin with one line of print written at the top of each page. • Change to one line of print on the left page, and one on the facing page. • Change to two lines of print per page if the child has control of the return sweep.
Captions	• Begin with caption books if necessary. • Change to books with sentences as soon as the child acquires more letters, sounds, and words. Reading sentences will let the child know that books tell a story. These books will also provide opportunities to rehearse simple sentence structures and practice fluent phrasing.
Punctuation	• Begin with a period. • If other punctuation marks, such as question marks and exclamation points, come up in conversation (and are then being used to create a book), use them in context and keep it simple. *I see a cat. Do you? Happy Birthday!*
Pictures	• Begin by placing the pictures in the same place on each page. Keep the pictures simple and make sure each picture supports the corresponding text. • Use a variety of pictures: photographs of the child, stickers (start a sticker collection), your own drawings, pictures cut from magazines and old workbooks, children's own drawings.
Letters and Words	• Keep a record of the letters and words the child can read and write. Include these in books you write for the child.

Directions for Making the Books

In addition to simply stapling paper together to make blank books, you can follow the steps provided here to make other easy books with children. Some lessons, such as for Pop-Up Books (page 54), require a specific book setup. Those directions are also included in this section.

Basic Books

1. For interior pages, fold several sheets of white paper in half (folding each sheet separately). Stack the folded papers with the folds facing right.

2. To make the cover, fold a new, thicker sheet of paper (tagboard or construction paper) in half. Place the fold to the left.

3. Place the inner pages inside the cover (folds still facing right) and staple along the left side to bind. Each folded sheet creates a page in the book (front and back), with a little more heft than a single sheet.

Teaching Tip

Consider precutting tagboard to make blank books. This sturdy paper comes in assorted colors and weights and can easily be cut from the standard 9- by 12-inch size to make pages for 6- by 9-inch books.

Basic Book-Making Materials

Following is a list of basic materials to have on hand for creating the books. Most of these are inexpensive and typically available in the classroom. Note that each lesson also includes a list of materials specific to the featured book(s).

- construction paper (white and assorted colors)
- glue sticks
- index cards
- library pockets (affixed to the back covers and used to hold manipulatives, such as letter cards)
- markers and crayons
- O-rings
- paper bags (see Mini Paper-Bag Books, page 58; also useful for gluing to the back of a book to hold letter, picture, and words cards)
- steno book or spiral notebook (see The Reflection Notebook, page 12)

- sticker collection
- scissors
- stapler
- sticky dots (for placing under each word in a sentence to encourage left-to-right directionality)
- tagboard in assorted colors (or other sturdy paper, such as manila)
- yarn

Note: It is also helpful to have a camera available for taking photographs of children and favorite activities. These photographs can serve as a springboard for many books.

Back-to-Back Books

1. Prepare each book page in advance, adding a blank page at the beginning and at the end. Then stack the book pages together, back to back. For example, place page 2 with its back to the back of page 1. Glue the pages in this manner back to back. Note that if you are making a pop-up book (see below), be careful not to glue this opening.

2. Stack the book pages on a larger sheet of construction paper or tagboard (or place inside a manila file folder).

3. Glue the front of the first page (blank) and the back of the last page (also blank) to the construction paper. Fold and staple along the edge to bind, then trim the cover to size.

Layer Books

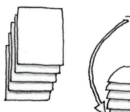

1. Stack several sheets of paper together and stagger them as shown (right).

2. Holding the paper securely, fold the top down to meet the bottom edge.

3. Crease at the fold and staple to bind.

Pop-Up Books

1. To make a cover for the book, fold a sheet of 9- by 12-inch construction paper in half.

2. To construct a pop-up page for a book, fold a sheet of 9- by 12-inch paper in half as shown, and cut as indicated to create a tab. (The illustration shows a one-tab pop-up page. Cut two tabs for a large pop-up or for more than one pop-up picture on a page.) Push the tab forward (in front).

3. Cut out a "pop-up" picture or shape. Glue the picture to the tab.

4. Create as many pop-up pages as you like, then stack the pages inside the front and back covers of the book. Staple to bind. For books with more than one pop-up page, glue the pages back to back. For example, glue the back (outside) of the top of pop-up page 2 to the back of the bottom of pop-up page 1. Note that for books with multiple pop-up pages, you can change the position of the pop-up picture by changing the placement of the tab. In this way, the picture "pops up" in a different place on each page, further drawing children's attention to pictures as visual support for text.

Teaching With the Lessons

Y ou can use the lessons in this book in any order that best meets your students' individual needs. For each lesson, you'll find the following components.

❋ **Reading Skills Support:** This section highlights benefits of each book, including ways in which it supports specific reading needs.

❋ **Materials:** This list identifies, in order of use, the materials you will need to construct a book. Most are inexpensive and readily available in classrooms. (Materials commonly used, such as glue sticks, pens, and staplers, are not included in these lists.) Note that the type of paper you use is flexible. If tagboard is specified, for example, you may use manila or other sturdy paper. Aim for durability so children can read their books again and again.

❋ **How to Make the Books:** These step-by-step directions explain how to construct each book, and include any special instructions, such as text and picture placement. Directions for making books in several different formats (such as pop-ups) are located on pages 8–9.

❋ **Teaching With the Books:** These guidelines for using the books with children include suggestions for reinforcing specific skills, such as print awareness and use of picture clues. Use these guidelines in conjunction with the mini-lesson on page 11, which provides suggestions for before, during, and after reading that can be adapted to any book.

❋ **Back-Cover Pocket Activity:** This optional activity provides a built-in extension for each book, in which a library pocket placed on the back cover holds a special activity for further skill practice.

❋ **Variations:** All of the books can be easily adapted to create an endless number of new books, to further reinforce a skill, to focus on a different topic or interest, or to add a new challenge. Unless otherwise noted, follow the basic book-making directions for the main lesson when constructing new titles.

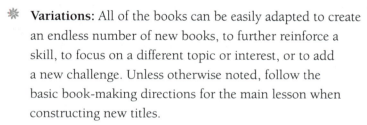

❋ **Literature Links:** These book suggestions feature favorite titles that can further support the goals of the lesson. Most of the books are readily available in school and public libraries. Others are selections from guided reading collections. If a book is not available, substitute a title with a similar level and features from another guided reading collection.

When preparing to use the books with children, it's helpful to think of the lesson like a conversation—the teacher and child talking, listening, noticing. "It seems from research that what is important for a good, natural learning situation is for the child to have a conversation with a person who uses simple language in correct forms and who is flexible enough to change his or her language to suit the language of the child being spoken to" (Clay, 1998, p. 6).

With this in mind, the goal of any lesson is to learn more about what the child knows, always looking for behaviors that show what the child can do. As you proceed with a lesson, move slowly from the known to the unknown. For example, if you are using a letter book with children (page 21), you will want to begin with known letters, setting aside blank pages to fill in at a later time as the child learns about more letters. With Cut-Up Sentence Books (page 68), begin with a child's dictated sentence (building familiarity into the written words). Later, a sentence from a piece of interactive writing, such as a response to a favorite read-aloud or class activity, might be appropriate.

Mini-Lesson: Before, During, and After Reading

In addition to the lesson included for each book, the mini-lesson here provides guidelines for before, during, and after reading. You can easily adapt these suggestions for use with any of the books you make for children.

Before Reading: Introduce the book, beginning with the cover. Read the title and invite the child to locate known letters and words. Then direct the child's attention to the picture (if there is one) and ask: "What do you notice?" Share a sentence or two about the book. Finally, teach a new story word or a word that is almost known, and rehearse tricky language structures.

During Reading: Model early reading behaviors, such as left-to-right directional movement. (See chart on page 6 for more information.) Say to the child, "Watch as I point to each word when I read. Now you follow me, by putting your finger next to mine." For a child with limited sense of story, read the book to the child first, then have the child read the book to you. Be ready to step in and help as needed.

After Reading: Ask questions and revisit pages to engage the child in a discussion about the book—for example, "What did you notice? Does this remind you of something? What is your favorite page? Why?" Reflect on the child's experience with the book. Ask yourself: What were some things the child could do independently? What could the child do with help? Use your observations and notes to plan for the next book you write for the child. (A Reflection Notebook, page 12, is a useful tool for these reflections.

Especially for English Language Learners

Books created just for children, with their abilities and interests in mind, are perfect for meeting the needs of English language learners. For example, make Storyboard Books (page 29) to extend a favorite theme, creating a whole picture for the child and a meaningful way to support second-language acquisition. The strong picture-word match in these books affords children opportunities to give names to things they recognize, building both oral language and word recognition. Encourage vocabulary-building conversations based on the books, again using the words and pictures as support.

The Reflection Notebook

The Reflection Notebook is a powerful assessment tool. Fast and "on the run," this "note-taking/note-making" approach provides a system for recording observations and immediately reflecting upon them (Dixon and Horn, 1995; Robertson, 1996; Yeager, 1999, as cited in Frank, 1999). A steno book works well for this purpose. These inexpensive pads have paper that is divided vertically in two sections. To set up and use a reflection notebook, follow these steps.

1. Label the left side "Note Taking." Label the right side "Note Making."

2. As you observe a child, take running records on the left side. For example, you might note words the child knows and words the child needs help with.

3. Record comments about your observations on the right side. These are your reflections about such things as the child's approach to unknown words, words the child can read, letters the child knows, tricky words, teacher prompts, and ideas for books based on the observations.

Useful Initial Vocabulary

Children need to build a core of basic words that they can read and write. Start with Marie Clay's "useful initial vocabulary," words that help with the first books a child can read (Clay, 1993). These words, with the addition of the child's name, all appear in the Dolch Sight Vocabulary 220 list, and all but one (*am*) are among the 150 most frequent words in printed school English, according to the *American Heritage Word Frequency Book* (Blevins, 2006).

[child's name]	come	is	my	to
a	go	it	on	up
am	here	like	see	
and	I	look	the	
at	in	me	this	

Teach the words as the child meets them in the reading, helping the child attend to the features of the letters in a word and understand how words work.

※ Use magnetic letters to construct the word on a magnetic whiteboard. Point to the first letter of the word. Point to the last letter of the word. Frame the word with your fingers.

※ Break apart the word and reassemble it. Write the word on the whiteboard or in a tray of colored sand.

※ Locate the word in the text. Now let the child try forming, reading, and writing the word.

※ Add the word to a word wall you create just for that child (for example, on chart paper or inside a file folder), and to the child's set of known-word cards.

Teaching Tip

Place a few known words in a library pocket you attach to the back of a familiar book. Have the child read or write the words quickly before reading.

Keep the following in mind as you choose books to create and develop lessons.

❋ Set aside a place to store materials for making books. Keep a file of photographs of children engaged in classroom activities and from special trips; these are good springboards for book topics. You might invite families to send in photos as well.

❋ Provide a place for children to store their special books. You can simply staple two sheets of tagboard together to make a portfolio. A 10- by 20-inch size will hold most books children will make, including Long Books (page 65).

❋ Keep a supply of simple, blank books on hand. (See pages 8–9 for directions for making different types of books.) At a moment's notice, you can then create a book for a child based on an observation or need.

❋ When making a book together with a child, keep your lesson in mind. If there is something you want to teach or discuss first, avoid distractions by setting aside stickers, scissors, markers, and other materials until you are ready to begin the actual book construction.

More Ways to Teach With the Books

As you use the books with children, you will discover ways of adapting them to create new books that address specific needs and reflect children's growing knowledge. The suggestions in this section are designed to help you create more books that will help children transition from teacher-made books to published guided reading material.

Concepts About Print

Using the front and back of the book, take opportunities to teach the following print awareness skills as needed.

❋ Letters can take many forms. Notice uppercase and lowercase letters, as well as different fonts, colors, and sizes.

❋ Words are made up of letters that go from left to right.

❋ Text can appear on a page with or without pictures.

❋ Words on a page correspond to speech.

❋ There are spaces between words in a group (such as in a caption or sentence). Discuss how these spaces help readers make sense of text.

❋ In the English language, words on the page are usually arranged in order from left to right and top to bottom.

❋ Attending to the punctuation is important: What is the period for? What is the question mark for?

❋ Stories have a beginning and an end.

Predictable Patterns

Many of the books you make will feature predictable patterns, which provide opportunities for overlearning "almost known words." Following is a starter list of predictable text that you can use to create an endless variety of books.

❋ [Child's name] is _____.

❋ I like _____.

❋ I can _____.

❋ I see _____.

❋ I am _____.

❋ A _____ can go _____.

❋ Run, _____, run.

❋ Look, a _____.

❋ Here is _____.

❋ Jump, _____, jump.

❋ Go, _____, go.

For the child who cannot follow a story, caption books are a beginning, a way to help the child feel like a reader. Caption books also utilize predictable patterns that you can vary from book to book.

❋ a _____

❋ an _____

❋ the _____

❋ two _____ (for a book about things that come in twos; or substitute other number words)

Dot Books

Dot books reinforce left-to-right directional movement and support one-to-one voice-print match. To use this strategy with any book that includes text, follow these steps.

1. Place a self-sticking green dot at the beginning of the line of text to show the child where to begin reading (Clay, 2005). Place a black dot or a pencil dot under each word.

2. As the child reads, have him or her touch each dot in turn. Make sure that the word the child points to matches what the child says.

Back-Cover Pocket Activities

A library pocket glued to the back of any book holds a special way for children to interact with the text (or pictures). See individual lessons for specific back-cover pocket extension activities. To incorporate this feature with other books you make, follow these steps.

1. Glue a library pocket to the back cover of the book.

2. In the pocket, place cards that children can manipulate and use with their book. Suggestions follow.

* To match letters in an alphabet book, include individual letter cards that children can match up to the corresponding pages in their book. Choose uppercase and lowercase letters in different fonts, colors, and sizes to help children develop an understanding of the many ways letters can look.

* To match words in sentences, provide cut-up sentence strips that students can rebuild on the pages of their book.

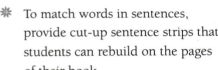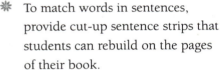

* Make word puzzles to reinforce key words. Write the words on index cards (one word per card) and cut between letters to create puzzle pieces.

Theme-Based Books

Child-centered themes are a great source of book topics. As you observe special areas of interest for children, consider using them as a focus for books you make together to extend a theme and build vocabulary. Pages 77–79 feature mini-lessons for making some of these theme-based books. Many of the books featured in the lessons can also be adapted to accommodate themes. Following are themes to consider.

Animals	Family	Oceans
Birthdays	Farm	Places
Bugs	Food	Plants
Colors	Friends	Transportation
Community	Human Body	Weather

When choosing a book format for a particular theme, consider your instructional goals for the child. For example, a pop-up format works well with "weather" words. The pop-up part of each page will draw children's attention to the picture. Change the position of the pop-up picture on each (see below) to further draw attention to the pictures. The sentence will draw the child's attention to the words, encouraging use of multiple cueing systems. Look for other theme-based suggestions throughout this book.

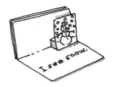

Interest Inventories

An interest inventory is a helpful resource for creating personalized books with children. Choosing topics you know are of interest to children builds motivation into every book.

1. Give each child a copy of the reproducible Interest Inventory: All About Me (page 17). Assist children as needed in completing the form.

2. Review the inventories with children to learn more about their interests. Keep these forms handy as you plan your book-making activities and lessons.

Bibliography

Blevins, W. (2006). *Phonics from A to Z* (2nd edition). New York: Scholastic.

Bodrova, E., & Leong, D. (1996). *Tools of the mind: The Vygotskian approach to early childhood education.* Englewood Cliffs, NJ: Prentice Hall.

Clay, M. M. (1991). *Becoming literate: The construction of inner control.* Portsmouth, NH: Heinemann.

_____. (1993). *Reading recovery: A guidebook for teachers in training.* Portsmouth, NH: Heinemann.

_____. (1998). *By different paths to common outcomes.* York, ME: Stenhouse.

_____. (2001). *Change over time in children's literacy development.* Portsmouth, NH: Heinemann.

_____. (2002). *An observation survey of early literacy achievement.* Portsmouth, NH: Heinemann.

_____. (2005a). *Literacy lessons designed for individuals, part one: Why? When? and How?* Portsmouth, NH: Heinemann.

_____. (2005b). *Literacy lessons designed for individuals, part two: Teaching procedures.* Portsmouth, NH: Heinemann.

DeFord, D. E., Lyons, C., & Pinnell, G. S. (Eds.). (1991). *Bridges to literacy: Learning from reading recovery.* Portsmouth, NH: Heinemann.

Dorn, L. J., French, C., & Jones, T. (1998). *Apprenticeship in literacy: Transitions across reading and writing.* York, ME: Stenhouse.

Frank, C. (1999). *Ethnographic eyes: A teacher's guide to classroom observation.* Portsmouth, NH: Heinemann.

Freeman, D. E., & Freeman, Y. S. (1994). *Between worlds: Access to second language acquisition.* Portsmouth, NH: Heinemann.

Leuenberger, C. J. (2003). *The new kindergarten: Teaching reading, writing & more.* New York: Scholastic.

Wink, J., & Putney, L. (2002). *A vision of Vygotsky.* Boston, MA: Allyn & Bacon.

Name: _____ Date: _____

All About Me

 Birthday: _____

 Pets: _____

 Family Members: _____
_____

Favorites

 Color: _____

 Stuffed Animal: _____

 Food: _____

 Game: _____

 Animal: _____

 Book: _____

 Place: _____

 School Subject: _____

 Sport: _____

 Season: _____

 Other: _____

Tracing Books

- colored construction paper (2 sheets; 9 by 6 inches each)
- white construction paper (3 sheets; 9 by 6 inches each)
- tracing paper (3 sheets; 9 by 6 inches each)
- black marker
- library pocket (optional)
- index cards (optional)

"This is the letter *g*. It goes around, up, down, and then it has a hook." For children learning to form letters, and for children who experience difficulty with this skill, tracing books provide personalized, guided practice in learning the shapes of letters. These tracing books motivate young learners by letting them trace letters in words that are naturally important to them—their own names. Tracing books build kinesthetic appeal into the learning experience, and add "the feel of movements to the child's sources of information" (Clay, 2005, p. 177).

Reading Skills Support

❋ Teach the shapes of letters through active exploration—in this case by tracing them.

❋ Provide support for children who are having trouble discriminating among letters, such as the direction of the extension in *b* and *p* or the left/right orientation in *d* and *b*.

❋ Provide for repeated letter-writing practice, which improves letter recognition (Clay, 1993; as cited in Blevins, 2006).

How to Make the Books

1. Print the child's name on one sheet of colored construction paper. This is the front cover of the book.

2. Using a black marker, print the child's name on each sheet of white construction paper.

3. Place a sheet of tracing paper on top of each sheet of white construction paper. Lay the cover on top, then place the remaining sheet of colored construction paper on the bottom (to create the back cover). Staple to bind the pages together.

Teaching With the Books

1. Share the book cover with the child and read the title (the child's name).

2. Trace the letters with your finger, modeling the direction of line and curve strokes while saying the name of each letter. Notice distinctive features of each letter, and point out differences among letters that are similar in some way. Let the child trace the letters with his or her finger, too, saying the name of each letter in turn.

3. Have the child use a pencil (or other writing instrument) to trace the letters in his or her name on the tracing paper on each page of the book. Encourage the child to say the name of each letter while tracing it.

Back-Cover Pocket Activity

A back-cover library pocket holds letter cards that invite further exploration of the book.

1. Glue a library pocket to the back cover of the book.

2. On an index card, write the child's name. If the tracing book features other words or letters, write these on index cards. Cut apart the card to create individual letter cards. Place the cards in the pocket.

3. Invite children to take out the cards and match them up to letters and words in the book.

Teaching Tip

Encourage children to say the letter names as they trace them. Offer support as needed to name unknown letters. Consider teaching memory devices, such as rhymes, to help children learn the features of different letters. Here's one for the letter *E*: "Pull straight down, just like me. Then slide to the right, one, two, three" (*Scholastic Spelling*, 1998; as cited in Blevins, 2006).

Follow the same format to create new tracing books.

❋ **Important Names Books:** What are other meaningful names in the child's life? Create tracing books that let children practice forming the letters in the names of people they know. From moms and dads to grandmas, grandpas, sisters, brothers, and babysitters, children's lives are full of important names they'll be motivated to learn.

❋ **Letter Books:** Write letters (uppercase, lowercase, or both) in the book, one letter per page.

❋ **Word Books:** Create tracing books based on sight-word or high-frequency word lists. Practicing these words will support letter knowledge and build sight word vocabulary, too.

Literature Links

Share alphabet books to provide further letter-recognition practice. Children can trace the letters in the books with their fingers to add a tactile element.

Alphabet Under Construction by Denise Fleming (Henry Holt, 2002): Young children will be inspired to create their own colorful alphabets after watching Mouse "construct" the letters from *A* to *Z*.

Max's ABC by Rosemary Wells (Puffin, reprint edition, 2008): "Max's ants escaped their ant farm," and they marched right over to Max for bites of his jelly sandwich. This alphabet adventure features favorite bunnies Max and Ruby, and reinforces letter recognition with one big, bright letter on each page. Each letter of the alphabet is further reinforced by boldfaced text in the target word (**A**nt).

Letter Books

Teach a few letters well, and it's amazing to see how this helps children learn them all. These books focus attention on individual letters—one letter per book—encouraging attention to distinct features, improving visual perception skills, and providing links that help children learn the sound commonly associated with each letter. As children are ready, follow the same format to create alphabet books that provide a picture link for every letter.

Reading Skills Support

❋ Repeated practice with individual letters encourages recognition of upper- and lowercase letter shapes.

❋ Pictures provide links between letters and sounds.

❋ The "letter-a-week" approach may not be appropriate for all children. These books focus attention on the letters children are having difficulty learning.

How to Make the Books

I. Staple paper together to make a basic blank book. (See bookmaking options on pages 8–9.)

2. Make multiple copies of the letter cards (unless writing letters by hand in the book).

3. Cut apart the letter cards. Glue one target letter card on the cover (or write the letter). A good place to begin is with the first letter of the child's name.

Materials

♦ colored construction paper (6- by 9-inch sheets)

♦ letter cards (pages 24–25)

♦ stickers or picture cards (pages 25–29)

♦ library pocket (optional)

♦ tagboard (optional)

4. On each page, glue the target letter card (or write the letter). To the right of the letter, place a sticker with an image that represents the sound commonly assigned to the letter. Or, use the picture cards provided (pages 25–29). For example, for the letter *Bb*, you could use stickers or picture cards for a ball, a balloon, and a bear. Because there are so few picturable words that begin with the letter *x*, picture cards are provided for *fox*, *box*, and *six*. Let children help select these pictures to create a stronger connection with their book.

Teaching With the Books

1. With the child, look at the cover of the book. Say the name of the letter and notice distinct features. For example, for a book about the letter *Dd*, you might notice both the straight line and the big curved line in the uppercase *D*, and the straight line and small circle in the lowercase *d*. Invite the child to trace the letters with his or her finger to add a tactile component.

2. Model how to read the book, looking at each "letter" page and saying the letter, then looking at the facing picture page and saying the name of the picture. Make a connection between the beginning sound of the picture word and the sound associated with the letter—for example, *dog* and /d/.

3. Let the child continue reading the book in the same manner, saying the name of the letter, looking at the picture, and saying the name for the picture. Encourage the child to listen for the letter sound at the beginning of the word.

Teaching Tip

When creating letter books, be sure to use the manuscript style children are learning— for example, Zaner-Bloser or D'Nealian.

Back-Cover Pocket Activity

A back-cover library pocket holds letter-card manipulatives that encourage further attention to the distinct features of the target letter.

1. Glue a library pocket to the back cover of the book.

2. Cut apart additional letter cards (pages 24–25), including the target letter and other letters the child knows. (For durability, glue to tagboard first if desired.) Cut apart each letter card to separate uppercase and lowercase letters.

3. Invite children to use letter cards to play sorting games. They can begin by sorting the letters into two groups: uppercase letters and lowercase letters. They can further sort those groups by letter features—for example, letters with straight lines only, letters with curved lines only, and letters with both straight and curved lines. Or, select the uppercase target letter and challenge the child to find the matching lowercase letter. Repeat to review other letters.

Variations

Follow the same format to create variations on the letter book.

* **Family Letter Books:** Create letter books featuring the first letter for family members' names (include their pictures, if possible).

* **Color Letter Books:** Build sound-letter relationships by creating letter books that feature favorite colors. On the left side of a spread, glue the letter card for the beginning of a color name. On the facing page provide a matching color swatch—and include the word naming that color.

* **Themed Letter Books:** Create letter books based on themed words. For example, a "seasonal" letter book might contain pictures that represent the current season, with the letter on each facing page to match. Sample letters and pictures for a fall letter book include *Ff* (fall), *Ll* (leaves), *Pp* (pumpkin), and *Hh* (Halloween). For winter, create pages for *Ww* (winter), *Ss* (snow), *Ii* (icicles), and *Mm* (mittens).

* **Alphabet Books:** Extend the books by creating a page for each letter of the alphabet.

Literature Links

Simple alphabet books provide children with more opportunities to encounter letters in different shapes and sizes and to practice letter recognition skills.

Alphabatics by Suse MacDonald (Aladdin, 1992): In this vibrant Caldecott Honor book, an *A* is turned upside down to become an ark and a blown-up *B* floats away as a balloon. The other letters also twist, turn, flip, and flop to become the objects they represent. Labels make connections among letters, sounds, and words.

Chicka Chicka Boom Boom by Bill Martin Jr. and John Archambault (Simon & Schuster, 1989): This colorful classic invites readers along as all the letters of the alphabet race to the top of the coconut tree.

Dr. Seuss's ABC by Dr. Seuss (Random House, 1996): Repetitive use of each letter and rhythmic text give children lots of practice with the alphabet.

Eating the Alphabet by Lois Ehlert (Harcourt, 1994): From "apple" to "zucchini," the colorful collage illustrations in this favorite book reinforce alphabet recognition with a feast of picture clues on every page.

26 Letters and 99 Cents by Tana Hoban (HarperCollins, 1987): Images of upper- and lowercase letters are matched to photographs of objects beginning with that letter, teaching letter recognition and building vocabulary. (The other half of this two-in-one book teaches numerals.)

A a	B b	C c
D d	E e	F f
G g	H h	I i
J j	K k	L l
M m	N n	O o
P p	Q q	R r

S s	**T t**	**U u**
V v	**W w**	**X x**
Y y	**Z z**	

  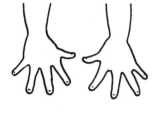

 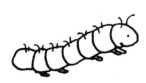 

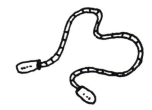

 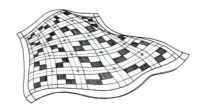 

 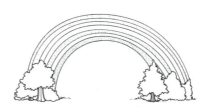 

  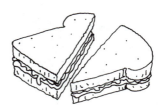

  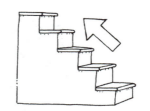

 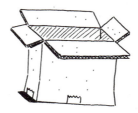 

Storyboard Books

Storyboard books take little scenes from life—a visit to a pond, dinner with a grandparent, a birthday party—and create opportunities for oral language development. Storyboard books are visually appealing, taking the shape of the book's subject (such as a big, red barn or a colorful birthday present) and building related language around that theme.

Materials

- Big, Red Barn storyboard template (page 32)
- word cards and picture cards (page 33)
- tagboard (12 by 18 inches)
- construction paper
- sentence strips
- colored tagboard (two colors, cut into approximately 3- by 3-inch squares)
- envelope (or lunch-size paper bag trimmed to about 5 inches high)

Reading Skills Support

❋ Storyboards build on what children know, using stories from their lives as sources for language development.

❋ Storyboards begin with something important to the child, and in this way provide natural links to children's literature, from which they can learn more.

How to Make the Books

Note: The directions and materials provided for this lesson are for a Big, Red Barn storyboard, inspired by the book *Big, Red Barn* by Margaret Wise Brown (HarperCollins, 1965). Use them as a model to create others based on children's interests and stories. (See Variations, page 31, for suggestions.)

1. Copy the Big, Red Barn template, word cards, and picture cards.

2. Glue the barn to a slightly larger sheet of tagboard. Color the barn red (or copy it on red paper), and add details as desired—for example, cut out colored construction paper to add a blue sky or green paper for grass.

3. Glue the picture and words cards to the colored tagboard squares (use one color for word cards and a different color for picture cards). Color the picture cards. Laminate all storyboard parts if desired.

4. Glue the envelope or lunch bag to the back of the barn. Place the picture and word cards inside. (Note that this lesson does not have a separate "Back-Cover Pocket Activity" because this feature is already part of the book.)

Teaching With the Books

1. Share a book about the topic, in this case farms, to help the child develop a framework for working with the storyboard. (See Literature Links, below, for suggested titles.) Say, "Let's take a closer look at the things we might see on the farm." Explore the book together, then introduce the storyboard.

2. Arrange the picture cards in a single row below the storyboard. Invite the child to name the pictures. Repeat with the word cards, having the child look for known words.

3. Revisit the picture cards. Say the name for each picture as you point to it. Let the child repeat the names for the pictures. Repeat with the word cards.

4. Let the child arrange the pictures on the storyboard, then match up the word cards. Offer assistance as needed. Ask questions to learn about the child's thought processes—for example, say, "These words both begin with the letter *c*. How did you know this word was *cow*?"

Variations

❋ **Pond Storyboard:** Create a storyboard that depicts a pond; make picture and word cards for plants and animals that live around a pond.

❋ **Happy Birthday! Storyboard:** Cut out a large tagboard gift-box shape and top with a bow. Make birthday-related picture and word cards.

❋ **Garden Storyboard:** On a sheet of tagboard, outline a garden scene. Make picture and word cards for things that grow or live in a garden.

❋ **Tree Storyboard:** Draw and cut out a large tree and glue to a sheet of tagboard. Make picture and word cards of animals that live in trees.

Teaching Tip

Start with picture and word cards. Add a cut-up sentence to the storyboard setup as children are ready. Write the sentence on a tagboard strip (or sentence strip) and cut it apart word by word. Children can assemble the sentence on the storyboard and read it. If appropriate, children can also write their own sentence to go with a storyboard, cut it apart, and assemble it.

Literature Links

Share books related to the storyboard topic to introduce children to related concepts and vocabulary.

Barn Dance! by Bill Martin Jr. and John Archambault (Henry Holt, 1988): A quiet barn comes alive one night as the animals dance to a scarecrow's fiddle music.

Farm Morning by David McPhail (Voyager, 1991): A young girl helps her father with the morning chores on their busy farm.

barn

cow	pig	horse
duck	hay	chicken
sheep	corn	tractor

Question Books

Materials

- sentence strips and word cards (page 38)
- picture cards (pages 39–41)
- tagboard (9- by 12-inch sheets, or cut to desired page size)
- photo of child
- library pocket (optional)
- index cards (optional)

"**W**here is Malik? Is Malik behind the tree?" "No!" Young readers often recognize the word *no*, which is included in the Dolch Basic Sight Vocabulary 220 and is among the 150 most frequent words in printed school English (Blevins, 2006). In fact, sometimes *no* is the only word a child can read! This book, an innovation on the classic *Where's Spot?*, by Eric Hill (Puffin, 1983), gives children plenty of practice with this familiar word to build fluency, and introduces new words through predictable text. With sentences that incorporate the child's name, pictures that support the text, and an irresistible lift-the-flap format, this book has immediate impact. Children are readers, actively engaged and attending to print.

Reading Skills Support

※ The question-answer format lets the teacher model reading behaviors when reading the questions, and gives the child a chance to practice those behaviors by reading the answers. (Teacher: "Is Malik behind the tree?" Child: "No!")

※ The use of questions and exclamatory text ("No!" and "Yes! Yes! Yes!") provide for fluency practice, letting children learn how to use inflection and expression in their reading.

※ Exposure to multiple sight words in each question and answer (such as *by*, *is*, *in*, *no*, *the*, and *yes*) helps children learn to more quickly recognize these words on their own, resulting in improved fluency.

How to Make the Books

1. Preview the reproducible sentence strips (page 38). Copy and cut them apart as follows:

* Where is _____?: Copy one strip for each book.

* Is _____ …?: Copy any four of these strips for each book (or another number depending on the length of the book you wish to make). You can repeat the same sentence strip—for example, "Is _____ under the _____?" or use a combination.

2. Copy and cut apart the word cards (three "No!" and three "Yes!") and four picture cards (pages 39–41). Color the picture cards for visual appeal. (You might invite children to do this in advance of making the book.)

3. Staple six sheets of tagboard together to make a book. (See pages 8–9 for other bookmaking options.) Use the following sample as a guide to put the book together. Glue a sentence strip on the left side of each spread. Glue the picture card on the right to create a flap. Complete the sentence by filling in the child's name and the name for the picture.

4. Under the first three picture flaps, glue the word "No!" (or "No! No! No!"). On the last page, under the final picture flap, glue a picture of the child and the words "Yes! Yes! Yes!"

Teaching Tip

With this book, you may wish to point out the different punctuation marks, and model for students how your voice changes with each. Children can notice how your voice goes "up" a bit when you read a sentence ending in a question mark. They can also practice using expression when reading the words "No!" and "Yes!"

Teaching With the Books

1. Share the cover and read the title. Point to each word in turn.

2. Read the first page—for example, "Where is Malik?" Point to each word as you read.

3. Turn the page and read the next question, pointing to the words in turn—for example, "Is Malik behind the tree?" Let the child lift up the picture on the facing page and point to and read the word "No!"

4. Repeat for the remaining pages, with the child lifting the flap and reading "Yes! Yes! Yes!" on the last page.

Back-Cover Pocket Activity

A back-cover library pocket holds word cards that invite further exploration of the question book.

1. Glue a library pocket to the back cover of the book.

2. Make word cards for known words such as *no* and *yes*. Place the word cards in the pocket.

3. When children are finished reading the book, invite them to take out the cards and match them to words in the book. As a variation, provide word cards for words in the book that match the pictures.

Variations

Use the child's Interest Inventory: All About Me (page 17) to generate a list of meaningful questions to use for variations on this book. In each case, follow the basic steps for the original book to create a new book. Sample questions follow.

❋ **Special Places:** Use a child's visit to a special place, such as the zoo, as the focus of a question book. The basic format from the original book doesn't change. ("Is [child's name] behind the [location]?") But this time, fill in the second blank with locations related to the specific place, and draw pictures that match (or use photographs if available), gluing them in place to create flaps the child can lift to reveal the text as with the original book.

❋ **Where Is [pet's name]?** If the child has a pet (or knows someone with a special pet) this question is a natural.

❋ **Where Is [lost object]?** Substitute a "lost" object, such as a sneaker. (Where is the <u>sneaker</u>? Is the <u>sneaker</u> in the <u>box</u>? Is the <u>sneaker</u> behind the <u>door</u>? Is the <u>sneaker</u> under the <u>bed</u>?)

❋ **_____, What Do You See?** Modeled after the classic *Brown Bear, Brown, Bear, What Do You See?* (see Literature Links, below), this book offers another variation on the question-answer format. The predictable response ("I see a _____ looking at me.") provides practice with multiple sight words.

❋ **Where's Caterpillar?** Modify the text pattern to support a study of insects. For example, generate a list of places where children might find a caterpillar. Use the list to write a set of questions (Is the caterpillar in the egg?, Is the caterpillar in the grass?, etc.) Create a lift-the-flap picture to go with each question, and construct the book as for the original. Glue a "No!" word card beneath each picture, until you reach the last page. Here, glue a picture of a caterpillar under the picture flap, along with a word card for "Yes! Yes! Yes!"

Literature Links

Each of the following books employs a question-answer format. Share them to invite children to make connections to their own question books. For fluency practice, invite children to chime in on predictable text, paying attention to punctuation marks and expression.

Brown Bear, Brown Bear, What Do You See? by Bill Martin Jr. (Harcourt Brace, 1967): Pre-readers easily pick up on the rhyming text pattern and can join in as they meet a new animal with every turn of the page.

Does a Kangaroo Have a Mother, Too? by Eric Carle (HarperCollins, 2000): Key words are highlighted in this colorful question-answer book about animal babies and their parents.

Have You Seen My Cat? by Eric Carle (Simon & Schuster, 1987): Repetitive text takes readers around the world as a young boy looks for his lost pet. Along the way, he meets many members of the cat family, including lions, tigers, and panthers, but each time he must reply, "This is not my cat!"

Where's Spot? by Eric Hill (Puffin, 1983): Young readers eagerly turn every page in search for Spot, who is late for dinner. Simple, repetitive text invites children to respond to the question-answer format.

Where is _____ ?

Is _____ behind the _____ ?

Is _____ under the _____ ?

Is _____ inside the _____ ?

No!	No!	No!	No!	No!
Yes!	Yes!	Yes!	Yes!	Yes!

Easy-to-Make Books That Target Specific Reading Needs © 2009 by Florence Miyamoto and Joan Novelli, Scholastic Teaching Resources

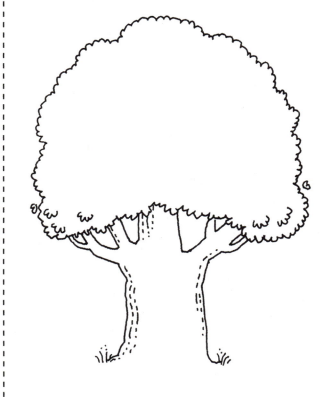

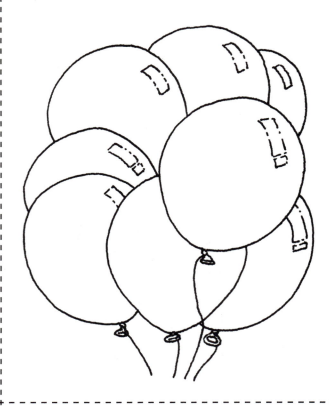

Easy-to-Make Books That Target Specific Reading Needs © 2009 by Florence Miyamoto and Joan Novelli, Scholastic Teaching Resources

Caption Books

For children who have a limited repertoire of known words, caption books provide positive independent reading experiences and create opportunities for the repeated practice that builds automaticity in word recognition. With only two to three words per page, these books are easy to customize for every child on any number of topics. From "school" and "friends" to "family," "pets," and "favorites," each book can incorporate words that are most meaningful for the child. By providing these manageable but motivating reading experiences, children are more likely to want to revisit the books and read new ones.

Reading Skills Support

✳ Captions are short and offer manageable chunks of text for readers with limited word knowledge.

✳ For those children who cannot follow a story, caption books make them feel like readers.

✳ Captions feature high-frequency words such as *a*, *an*, *the*, and *one*. Learning to recognize these words quickly is necessary for fluent reading.

✳ Being able to read words that are important to them increases children's motivation and success.

How to Make the Books

1. Place tagboard pages between construction-paper covers and bind to make a blank book. (See pages 8–9 for other bookmaking options.)

2. With the child, decide on a topic. The child's Interest Inventory: All About Me (page 17) may be a source of ideas. Write the title—for example, "Parker's Book of Animals," on the cover.

3. Have the child select pictures to go with the topic. Glue these in the book, one per page. Glue a caption strip beneath each picture and write in the word that names that picture. Or, in place of using the caption templates, simply write the corresponding caption—for example, "a cat"—beneath each picture.

4. End the caption book with a sentence that goes with the story, to add meaning to the story.

Teaching With the Books

1. Read the cover with the child. Help the child with any unknown words.

2. Turn to the first page and review the word or words that will repeat on each page—for example, the word *a* in "a cat." Let the child read the first page. If needed, remind the child to use the picture as a visual reminder of at least one of the words on the page.

3. Have the child continue reading, looking at each picture to confirm the caption.

4. Have the child make a known word with magnetic letters, break the word apart, and assemble it again. Let the child write the word in the air, on his or her hand, or on a whiteboard with a dry-erase marker, then locate the word in the story.

Teaching Tip

Pages 45–46 provide caption strips and pictures you can use to create caption books. The captions are generic ("a _____," "my _____," and so on) and can be used to make many different caption books.

Back-Cover Pocket Activity

A back-cover library pocket holds word cards for matching up to words in the book, reinforcing word recognition skills.

1. Glue a library pocket to the back cover of the book.

2. Cut index cards into four equal pieces (to create smaller word cards). On each index-card section, write a word from the book. For words that appear more than once, create a card for each word.

3. Place the word cards in the pocket.

4. When children are finished reading the book, invite them to take out the word cards and arrange them to make each caption in the book. When they are finished, they can read the captions they made.

Variations

Let children lead the way when it comes to variations on the caption book. They will have their own ideas about the topics that are important to them. With this in mind, some suggestions follow.

✳ **All Around the School Caption Books:** Take photographs of places around the school. Glue a photo to each page and write a caption—for example, "the office," "the library," "the lunchroom," "the classroom," and "the playground."

✳ **My Classmates Caption Books:** Create caption books that simply name children in the class. Children can share these at home so that families can get to know who's who in the classroom.

✳ **Weather Words Caption Books:** Glue weather pictures in a book and provide a descriptive caption for each—for example, "a sunny day" or "a snowy day."

✳ **Color Caption Books:** Create caption books that describe objects by color— for example, "a red fire truck," "a blue bicycle," "a green frog," and "a yellow dog." Include a picture of each object in the corresponding color.

✳ **My Friends Caption Books:** Create caption books that feature a child's special friends. Place a photograph of a friend on each page and write a caption that names that child: "my friend [child's name]."

✳ **Counting Caption Books:** Let the child place stickers from 1 to 10 on each page. (Be sure the stickers on each page are the same, but they can differ from page to page.) Write a caption for each that tells how many: "1 bug," "2 bugs," "3 bugs," and so on.

Literature Links

Share books that feature captions to encourage children to make connections between their own caption books and other books.

The Birthday Cake by Joy Cowley (Wright Group, 1993): It's the queen's birthday and the royal bakers are making a colorful layered cake for her: ". . . a red cake, a yellow cake, a blue cake…"

The New Cat by Joy Cowley (Learning Media Limited, 1997): In this story, readers meet "Greedy" cat for the first time as a new kitten. He has an insatiable appetite for food, gobbling up everything he sees: "The milk. Gobble, gobble. The fish. Gobble, gobble. The bread. Gobble, gobble."

The Seed by Christine Young (Wright Group, 1993): "A seed, a plant, a flower . . ." This beautifully illustrated caption book tells the life cycle of a seed.

a _____   an _____

a _____   an _____

a _____   an _____

a _____   an _____

a _____   an _____

my _____

the _____

my _____

the _____

my _____

the _____

my _____

the _____

my _____

the _____

Name Books

"**H**ere are the letters in your name: *A-n-t-h-o-n-y*. Point to the first letter. Point to the last letter. . . ." The most powerful known word for a child is his or her name. From the construction of the child's name comes an understanding that letters come together in a certain way. A book that features a child in photographs creates meaningful reasons to repeat that important word on every page.

Reading Skills Support

❋ Names provide motivating opportunities to teach uppercase and lowercase letters and concepts about print, such as the left-to-right sequence of letters in words and the space between words.

❋ A name is usually a known or almost known word for the child. Placed strategically at the beginning of a sentence, the child's name in print builds success into the reading experience: The child can start the sentence with a known word, which provides motivation and encourages confidence.

❋ Names provide opportunities for wordplay—for example, looking for little words and big words within a child's name.

Highlighting tape is removable transparent tape that comes in different colors and can be placed on a word to make it pop. With these name books, highlighting tape placed over a child's name brings attention to this special word. Place it over the child's name on the cover, and the child can remove it and use it on each text page to highlight his or her name again. Consider using highlighting tape with any of the books you make to draw attention to certain features of the book—a word, the beginning of a sentence, and so on.

How to Make the Books

1. Take photographs of the child engaged in everyday activities, such as reading a book, writing, painting a picture, or eating lunch.

2. To make a blank book, cut sheets of tagboard (or construction paper) to the desired size. Punch two or three holes on the left side of each sheet and use O-rings to bind. (This construction will make it easy to add pages to the book at a later time.)

3. Invite the child to help title the book. (Make sure the title incorporates the child's name.) Write the title on the cover and invite the child to illustrate.

4. Open the book to the first interior page and affix a photo to it, leaving room above or below to write a sentence. Write a simple sentence that starts with the child's name and describes what the child is doing—for example, "Anthony is eating lunch." Repeat this procedure on a new page for each photo, using consistent placement of the sentence.

Teaching With the Books

1. Look at the cover together and notice the child's name. Say the name for each letter and point to it. ("Here are the letters in your name, *A-n-t-h-o-n-y*.") Invite the child to point to the first letter, then to the last letter. Model how to frame the name with your fingers (or use highlighting tape). Point out that the name begins with an uppercase letter, and make note of letters the child knows and those the child needs to learn.

2. Turn to the first spread and look at the text and the picture. Read the sentence on the left page together (or model for the child), pointing out how the picture helps you make sense of the text. Continue with each page, or let the child read independently, if appropriate.

Back-Cover Pocket Activity

A back-cover library pocket holds letter cards that spell a very important word: the child's name.

S a m

1. Glue a library pocket to the back cover of the book.

2. Write the child's name on an index card and cut it apart letter by letter.

3. Place the letter cards in the pocket. When children are finished reading the book, invite them to take out the letter cards and use them to spell their name.

Variations

There is no end to books you can make that feature a child's name. By maintaining the use of the child's name (a known word) in each sentence, you can keep the familiar while incorporating new words as the child is ready.

❋ **Glitter Books:** Simply writing the child's name with a glitter pen (or outlining with glitter glue) adds enormous appeal to any name book.

❋ **Family Books:** Invite families to send in a few photos of the child with each family member (and the family pet). Use the photos to make a book about the child's family. Maintain use of the child's name in the predictable text structure—for example, "Anthony has a sister" or "Anthony has a dog."

❋ **Memory Books:** Transform a few photos from home into a book the child will read again and again. Invite families to send in photos of memorable moments—a child's first birthday, first step, first day of school, and so on. Use a predictable text pattern that features the child's name and tells what is happening in each photo—for example, "Louisa is 1!" "Louisa is walking!" and "Louisa is riding a bike!"

Literature Links

Introduce children to some favorite storybook characters who have special names of their own.

Chrysanthemum by Kevin Henkes (Greenwillow, 1991): Young Chrysanthemum discovers that her name is as big as "… half the letters in the alphabet!" Her name, a source of some teasing by kindergarten classmates, becomes a special source of pride when her music teacher decides to give her new baby the same "absolutely perfect" name.

Corduroy by Don Freeman (Viking, 1968): Set in a department store, this beloved story tells the adventures of a teddy bear who climbs off the shelf to go in search of a missing button. A young girl who purchases the bear gives him a new button and names him after the overalls he wears.

Madeline by Ludwig Bemelmans (Viking, 1967): This timeless tale (a Caldecott Honor winner) introduces Madeline, a young girl who lives with 11 other girls and Miss Clavel in a home in Paris. Rhyming text invites young children to chime in.

Olivia by Ian Falconer (Atheneum, 2000): The endearing heroine of this book wears only red and is "very good at wearing people out." Children are sure to get to know this character's name very quickly. *Olivia Forms a Band* and *Olivia Saves the Circus* are among other titles in this favorite series.

Photograph-Based Books

Materials

- tagboard
- photographs
- O-rings
- photo corners (or double-stick tape or glue stick)
- library pocket (optional)
- index cards (optional)

Classroom and family photographs hold special meaning for children. Photographs invite children to name familiar people and places and, with these connections in place, make it easier to learn to recognize these names and words in print. With these books, which naturally follow the Name Books (page 47), predictable text reinforces word knowledge, and snapshots provide strong visual clues to any unknown words in the text.

Reading Skills Support

- Photographs provide an already established sense of story, which helps children make sense of print.
- For English language learners, these picture books provide important visual clues for building vocabulary.
- For children having trouble learning high-frequency words, the pictures encourage "associative learning." By associating the target words ("I can see a …") with a picture ("… cat.") on each page, children may more easily "store" knowledge of the words (Blevins, 2006).
- Knowledge of high-frequency words, which can be included, improves reading fluency.

How to Make the Books

I. Cut sheets of tagboard (or construction paper) to make book pages. Punch two or three holes along the left side of each sheet (line up the holes in each sheet first) and use O-rings to bind the pages.

2. Create a cover for the book. Write the book title (such as "My Family") and invite the child to draw a picture.

3. Work with the child to select and sequence several photos for the book. These can be photos from home or of the child at school. Affix a photo to each page, using photo corners or double-stick tape.

4. Together with the child, write a sentence on each page that describes the photograph—for example, "I can see my sister." Choose high-frequency words and phrases ("I can see my…") that you can repeat for each photograph.

Teaching With the Books

I. Look at the cover with the child. Read the title together and notice the picture. Model pre-reading strategies—for example, wonder aloud what this book is about. Having selected meaningful photographs to illustrate the book, the child will be eager to help answer.

2. Let the child read each page. Offer assistance with text as needed and encourage children to use the pictures as visual clues for any unknown words.

Back-Cover Pocket Activity

A back-cover library pocket holds new photographs and captions for children to match up.

I. Glue a library pocket to the back cover of the book.

2. Choose several new photographs and write a caption on index cards to go with each. (Use the same predictable text pattern on the cards as in the book.)

3. Place the photographs and captions in the pocket. When children are finished reading the book, invite them to take out the new photographs and captions and match them up.

Teaching Tip

As the child is able, you might revisit words in the book that name people or objects in the photographs. Have the child name the subject of the picture, then find the matching word. Encourage the child to use sound-letter knowledge to identify these words. For example, if the child sees his or her dog in a picture, point out that *dog* begins with /d/. Ask: "What letter goes with /d/? Which word is *dog*?"

I can see my bedroom.

Variations

❋ **Caption Books:** To simplify the books, write short captions rather than complete sentences—for example, "my cat," "my cubby," or "my birthday cake."

❋ **Family Photo-Album Books:** Start a family photo album that the child can add to at school. Introduce new predictable text patterns over time, as appropriate.

❋ **Themed Photo Books:** With the child, sort photographs by theme—for example, pictures about a pet, a birthday party, or a class trip. Use the photographs to create themed picture books.

❋ **Stick-On Sentence Books:** Add words to favorite books by Tana Hoban. Choose a wordless book by this author (see Literature Links for a few suggestions) and write simple sentences on tagboard strips to go with each page. Let children match the sentences to the photographs. With removable wall adhesive, they can stick the captions right to the page, then read the book.

Literature Links

Look for books with similar features to share with children. Books with photographs in particular will let children make connections between the books they made and other books they can read.

Dad by Beverley Randell, Jenny Giles, and Annette Smith (Rigby, 1996): Part of the guided reading series PM Starters One, this book features photographs that show "Dad" at work and play. The simple, patterned text and consistent layout of the print provide a good example for creating photo books.

Faces by Janie Everett (Scott, Foresman, 1993): Photographs in this book, part of the Little Celebrations guided reading series, capture the faces and feelings of childhood. Combined with simple, predictable text, the photos serve as inspiration for a class photo album that children will be drawn to read again and again.

Is It Larger? Is It Smaller? by Tana Hoban (HarperCollins, 1997): Photographs invite children to explore the concept of size and provide opportunities on every page to learn words to name what they see.

Is It Red? Is It Yellow? Is It Blue? by Tana Hoban (HarperCollins, 1987): This wordless picture book invites children to name the colors they see.

Look Book by Tana Hoban (Greenwillow, 1997): "Peek-through" pages let children view a small part of a photograph to guess the object. Pictures will inspire interest in learning new words like *pretzels* and *pigeon*.

I can see a _____.

I can see an _____.

I can see my _____.

I can see our _____.

I can see the _____.

Pop-Up Books

- pop-up template (page 57)
- plain paper
- several sheets of construction paper (or tagboard)
- themed stickers (such as "farm" or "animals")
- glue (if using pictures other than stickers)

Pop-up books are easy to make and lots of fun to read, and they serve the instructional purpose of encouraging the child to stop and look at the picture. This is an important strategy for young children to learn—that pictures and words in a book work together, and that they can use pictures to figure out unknown words and better understand what's happening.

Reading Skills Support

✸ Young readers benefit from using pictures as visual clues to figure out unknown words in a text.

✸ The pop-up format naturally draws the child's attention to the picture on the page, serving as a reminder that pictures are one of the tools readers use to bring meaning to a text.

How to Make the Books

1. Copy and cut out the pop-up book template. Then fold each page on the center line and cut on the dashed lines to create the tab. Push the tab forward (into the page).

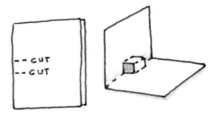

2. Choose a sticker and place it on a piece of colored construction paper (cut to frame the sticker). Glue the paper to the pop-up tab.

3. Repeat step 3 to create as many pop-up pages as you like, then place the pages inside a construction-paper front and back cover. Staple to bind.

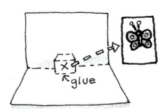

4. Glue the interior pages back to back. For example, glue the back (outside) of the top of pop-up page 2 to the back of the bottom of pop-up page 1.

5. Write a sentence about each sticker under the picture.

6. Write the title on the cover page and invite the child to add an illustration (or choose a sticker to place on the cover).

Teaching With the Books

1. With the child, look at the cover and read the title. Then begin reading the book with the child. Turn to the first page and notice the picture that pops up. Allow time for the child to respond to this surprise on the page. Explain that pictures are clues that help readers figure out words. Invite the child to describe the picture. What does it show?

2. Guide the child in reading the sentence, using the picture to figure out (or check) any unfamiliar words. Pause to talk about connections the child makes between the words and the picture.

3. Repeat for each additional page. Reinforce the connections on each page between the picture and the words.

Back-Cover Pocket Activity

A back-cover library pocket holds pictures and sentences for the child to match, reinforcing the connection between pictures and words on the page.

1. Glue a library pocket to the back cover of the book.

2. Select several new stickers and place them on index cards (one sticker per index card). Write a sentence about the sticker underneath it. Cut apart each index card to separate the sticker from the sentence.

3. Place the stickers and sentences in the pocket. When the child is finished reading the book, invite him or her to take out the cards and match up each sticker with a sentence. (For self-checking, use different-color sticky dots to color-code each picture-sentence pair. For example, place a green sticky dot on the back of each part of one sticker-sentence set, red on another, and so on.)

Teaching Tip

When discussing how readers use pictures as clues to figure out unknown words, remind children of other strategies they can use when they get stuck. This might include, for example, looking for little words in big words and using what they know about letters and sounds to make a good guess (then checking to see if it makes sense).

Variations

❋ **Alphabet Pop-Up Books:** Make pop-up pages for each letter you want to include in the book. Copy and cut apart the letter and picture cards on pages 24–28. Place a picture on the pop-up tab for each page ("frame" it on a piece of colored construction paper first, if desired), and glue the letter card beneath. You might also write the name that corresponds to the picture (and letter), if desired.

❋ **Favorite Pop-Up Books:** Let children dictate sentences about things they like, such as "I like cats." Use their sentences to make pop-up books. Draw or cut out pictures from magazines or old workbooks to go with their sentences. Glue the pictures to the pop-up tabs and copy the sentences beneath.

❋ **Photo Pop-Up Books:** Invite families to send in photos of their child. Encourage them to select photos that show their child engaged in something specific (that can be named in a sentence), such as playing ball or visiting with a grandparent. Use copies of the photos for the pop-up pictures.

❋ **Storybook Pop-Up Books:** Read a class favorite and make a class pop-up about the characters or events.

Literature Links

To encourage children to notice illustrations and make the connection between pictures and text, look for books, such as those that follow, that feature out-of-the-ordinary formats.

Alpha Bugs: A Pop-Up Alphabet by David A. Carter (Little Simon, 2006): In this innovative alphabet book, familiar objects such as a waffle iron are embellished with eyes, antennae, and other details to create bubble bugs, jelly-bean bugs, and more. Pop-ups, pull tabs, and flaps add to the fun. Look for other pop-up books by this author.

Color Surprises: A Pop-Up Book by Chuck Murphy (Simon & Schuster, 1997): "Can you guess what's hiding behind each color?" Children lift the colored squares to discover a surprising link to each color word.

Papa, Please Get the Moon for Me by Eric Carle (Simon & Schuster, 1991): In a story that teaches the lunar phases, a young girl asks her father to bring her the moon. To the delight of young readers, the book features pages that fold out and up, so when Papa goes to get a ladder to fetch the moon, the page opens out (to show the ladder), up (to climb the ladder), and out again for a splendid view of the full moon.

Mini Paper-Bag Books

- small paper "party" bags (5- by 9-inch; available in bright colors at craft stores)
- construction paper
- tagboard (cut into 1- by 7-inch sentence strips)
- letter cards (pages 24–25)
- stickers (or pictures)
- library pocket (optional)

These playful mini paper-bag books have big appeal for young children. Each page in the book is a small bag, on the outside of which is text (a letter, word, or sentence) and a picture. Inside each bag are surprises for the reader to discover—letter and word manipulatives, a photo, stickers, even a little treat. It's easy to restock the bags every now and then with fresh manipulatives, bringing children back to see what's new—and in the process gaining the repeated practice they need to become strong readers.

Reading Skills Support

✻ Exploring letters, sounds, and words in a playful way is a natural reading motivator.

✻ Active exploration helps build a thorough knowledge of the alphabet, making it easier for children to learn sound-spelling relationships.

✻ The use of manipulatives supports children who learn best through a kinesthetic and tactile approach.

How to Make the Books

1. Stack four to five paper bags and staple at the bottom. Turn the book horizontally, so the bag bottoms are on the left. The bag openings are now on the right and the pages turn in the same way as a standard book.

2. Select a focus for the book and choose an appropriate, predictable text pattern. The following examples provide an idea of the many directions you can go with these books. Rather than writing text directly on the paper bags, write the title and sentences on tagboard strips and then attach these to the paper-bag pages. If desired, cut apart the strips word by word (punctuation, too) and glue in order on the page, leaving a small amount of space between each.

Birthdays: Celebrate children's special day with a birthday book.

❋ Write a title on the cover (first bag), such as "Birthdays." Add an appealing birthday sticker or picture.

❋ On each interior page, use a predictable text pattern to write a story about birthdays. Sample text for a four-page book follows: *I like balloons. Do you?/ I l like cake. Do you?/ I like presents. Do you?/ I like birthdays! Do you?* Inside each bag, place a surprise. The first bag (cover) may hold a birthday card for the child and a small treat, such as a bookmark or sparkly sticker. Other bags may hold word cards to match to the sentence on the page or, in the case of the sample (above), "Yes" and "No" word cards the child can place on the page to answer the question ("Do you?").

Favorites: Make a book about a child's favorite things.

❋ Write the child's name on the cover (first bag). Decorate with stars, a picture, or another appealing visual.

❋ On each interior page, use a predictable text pattern to name the child's favorites—for example: *I like cats. Do you?/ I like ladybugs. Do you?/ I like seashells. Do you?* Use stickers or pictures to illustrate each page. Inside the first bag (cover), place letter cards that spell the child's name and a picture of the child.

❋ For other pages, you might place word cards that answer a question in the text (for the sample above, the word "Yes") or letter cards to spell target words, such as *ladybugs*.

Teaching Tip

Place letter cards and other manipulatives in small (2 ½- by 3-inch) envelopes (available at craft and office-supply stores) before placing inside the bags.

Children will want to revisit these special books often. To keep the learning going, add fresh surprises to the bags now and then, based on the child's skills and new challenges that may be appropriate. For example, inside a bag in the "Favorites" book (see page 59), it may be appropriate to place letter cards that spell *ladybugs*, and invite the child to manipulate them to make new words, such as *day, say, dug,* and *slug.*

Friends: This book about friends reinforces sound-spelling relationships.

✻ Write a title on the cover (first bag), such as "Kevin's Friends." Outline the first letter with puff paint or yarn to make it stand out.

✻ On the first interior page, write a predictable text pattern that lets the child fill in the first letter of his or her name: *Kevin's name starts with* _____. (Highlight the first letter of the name in a different color.)

✻ Repeat on remaining pages, substituting the names of friends.

✻ Place a picture of the child on each page, and place the letter card that fills in the blank inside the bag.

Teaching With the Books

1. Together with the child, read the title on the cover. Invite the child to tell what he or she knows about the letters or words, such as the different shapes that make up the letters or the sounds that go with the letters. Which words are known?

2. Guide the child in exploring each page, beginning with the cover. For "Kevin's Friends," for example, you might begin by taking a closer look at the name on the cover, beginning with the first letter, *K*: "Trace it with your finger. It goes down, then in, then out."

3. Proceed with each page in the book, reading the text, looking at letters and words, exploring concepts about print (such as the space between words), making connections to the picture, and exploring the surprise inside each bag.

Back-Cover Pocket Activity

A back-cover library pocket holds a paper bag for children to make a new "page."

1. Glue a library pocket to the back cover of the book.

2. Inside the pocket, place a small paper bag (the same size as for the original book).

3. Provide materials, such as construction paper, letter cards, and stickers, and invite the child to create a new page based on the book, complete with a surprise inside.

4. Invite the child to read the new paper-bag page with you.

Variations

❊ **Letter Books:** To focus on letter recognition and sound-letter relationships, glue target letter cards (see pages 24–25) on each bag, along with a sticker that represents that letter. Inside the bags, place pieces of Wikki Stix™ (colorful waxed yarn). Children can use the Wikki Stix™ to form the letter (on top of the letter in the book), then trace it with their finger.

❊ **Add-a-Puzzle Books:** Choose an important word from a sentence on each page (for example, a friend's name from the "Friends" book), and make a word puzzle to go with it. Write the word on a colorful tagboard strip, and cut it apart letter by letter into jigsaw puzzle pieces. Place each puzzle in the corresponding bag, along with a matching picture (or photo).

❊ **Themed Books:** Choose a unit of study, such as weather, and create paper-bag books to support children in learning more. Use the bags to reinforce vocabulary—for example, using predictable text patterns that incorporate weather words children are learning—for example, "Look at the rain" and "Look at the clouds." Add pictures to match the text on each page, and in the bags place word puzzles children can put together to spell their weather words.

Literature Links

Books with movable parts appeal to a young child's hands-on approach to learning and encourage an excitement about reading. Read these books with children, making connections between the visuals and the words, or just let them have fun exploring the interactive construction.

The Jolly Postman by Janet and Allan Ahlberg (Little, Brown, 2001): The Jolly Postman goes from house to house delivering the mail to "addresses" children will recognize from familiar fairy tales and nursery rhymes. This enchanting book has pages with envelopes that contain letters children can take out and read—including one from Goldilocks to Baby Bear!

My Little Yellow Taxi by Stephen T. Johnson (Red Wagon, 2006): This inventive book puts young children in the driver's seat of a shiny yellow cab, complete with 16 interactive features that let them get ready to go. There's a mirror to adjust, tire pressure to check, an engine to start, and more. *My Little Red Toolbox*, by the same Caldecott Honor artist, is just as much fun.

Puzzle Books

- construction paper (9- by 12-inch sheet)
- tagboard (6- by 9-inch sheets)
- sentence strips
- envelopes (letter size)
- magnetic letters (or letter tiles)
- library pocket (optional)
- index cards (optional)

Puzzle books are like little snapshots of a child's thinking, providing opportunities to observe what the child does when faced with a problem. A page in a puzzle book can hold a picture, a word, or a sentence— each cut into puzzle pieces.

Reading Skills Support

✳ Reading requires children to figure things out—as with a puzzle. Puzzle books provide a playful way to explore problem solving related to letters and words.

✳ The puzzle format provides kinesthetic and tactile learners with opportunities for active learning.

✳ Puzzles made with names and other words reinforce that letters come together from left to right in a certain sequence to make words. The same is true for puzzles made with sentences.

How to Make the Books

1. Fold the construction paper in half to create a 6- by 9-inch front and back cover. Stack the tagboard sheets horizontally and place inside the construction paper. Staple to bind. (This book will be created with the fold, or binding, at the top; pages will open up.)

2. Write the child's name on a sentence strip or colored tagboard. Cut the name apart letter by letter to create jigsaw puzzle pieces.

3. Place the puzzle pieces in an envelope. Glue the back of the envelope to page 1 in the book. Label the envelope with the child's name.

4. Repeat the puzzle-making process with other words that are important to the child. (Invite the child to choose these.) Place each set of puzzle pieces in an envelope and glue to a page in the book.

5. Write a title on the cover ("[child's name]'s Puzzle Book").

Teaching With the Books

1. Model the process for "reading" the book: remove puzzle pieces from an envelope and think aloud as you put them together. Mention clues you use to decide the correct position for each piece—for example, a capital letter comes at the beginning of a name.

2. Say the name and listen for the ending sound. Think aloud about how to find the letter that matches that sound and where it goes (to the right, where the end of the name will be).

3. Let the child take a turn with the same puzzle, then continue on together, or, if appropriate, the child can work independently. Notice strategies the child uses to determine how the pieces fit together.

4. Give the child magnetic letters (or letter tiles) to make a known word from a puzzle—for example, the letters in the child's name. Have the child arrange the letters to spell his or her name. Then break apart the word and invite the child to form it again.

Teaching Tip

Careful note taking is key with these puzzle books. Watch carefully for subtle changes over time and slowly move the child from name puzzles (or letter puzzles, if appropriate) to other word puzzles and finally to cut-up sentence puzzles. (See Variations, page 64.)

Back-Cover Pocket Activity

A back-cover library pocket holds a surprise puzzle for the child.

1. Glue a library pocket to the back cover of the book.

2. Make a puzzle that will reveal a special surprise for the child. You might, for example, write the child's name in glitter and include a special sticker as part of the puzzle.

3. Cut the puzzle into pieces and place in the pocket. Include a tagboard card onto which the child can glue the completed puzzle.

Variations

✳ **Letter Puzzle Books:** To reinforce letter recognition, write uppercase and lowercase letter pairs on tagboard and cut apart into jigsaw-puzzle pieces to separate by uppercase and lowercase.

✳ **Classmate Puzzle Books:** Make a class book of puzzles featuring a name puzzle for each child. Place a picture of each child on the envelope holding that child's name puzzle.

✳ **Color-Word Puzzle Books:** Create color-word puzzles, using cardstock that matches the color (or glue matching construction paper to tagboard, and use to make the puzzles).

✳ **Animal-Name Puzzle Books:** Make word puzzles featuring the names for favorite animals. Add a sticker or other picture to these puzzles for added appeal.

✳ **Number-Word Puzzle Books:** Make puzzles that teach number words. Use the words only, or combine the words with the numeral and a matching set of objects.

Literature Links

To extend the idea of problem solving when reading, choose books from your guided reading collections that introduce sight words in simple repetitive phrases using the language structure of the child. Following are several examples; or choose other books with similar features.

Hello, Bingo! by Jenny Giles, Beverley Randell, and Annette Smith (Rigby, 2006): Simple language structures such as "Come and look." and "Here is…" invite the reader into this story about a girl and her mother who are looking for a dog to take home. Key phrases repeat and tricky words such as *come* and *here* are seen and read again and again.

Sally and the Elephant by Jenny Giles, Beverley Randell, and Annette Smith (Rigby, 2006): The words *look*, *can*, and *see* appear repeatedly in this story about Sally and her mom's day at the zoo. Patterned text and consistent print layout provide many opportunities for the reader to see and say these sight words.

Sally and the Leaves by Jenny Giles, Beverley Randell, and Annette Smith (Rigby, 2006): Patterned text with strong picture support introduce the color words *red*, *green*, *yellow*, and *brown* in a story about Sally and her mom, who are collecting leaves at the park.

Long Books

"**P**ut your finger next to mine, and follow along as we read the story together. . . ."
With sentences that stretch across a long, horizontal page, these books are a perfect way to provide young readers with the practice they need to develop early reading behaviors. (See page 6 for more information on specific reading behaviors.)

Reading Skills Support

* With an unusual and eye-catching design, long books build motivation into the reading process.

* The format supports acquisition of concepts about print, including left-to-right directionality, and allows for exaggerated spaces between words, which helps children recognize "word boundaries" and supports the understanding of voice-print match.

* Predictable text supports children in developing print awareness, builds confidence, and provides practice in saying and hearing simple language structures in their growing skills.

How to Make the Books

1. Fold the construction and manila paper in half horizontally. Place the manila paper inside the folded construction paper (so folds meet) and staple to bind. (These are horizontal books, stapled at the top.)

2. Choose a topic with the child. Check the child's interest inventory (page 17) for ideas. Provide stickers or other pictures related to that topic and let the child select several to illustrate the pages of the book. (Or have the child draw several pictures or cut them from magazines.)

3. Write a title on the construction-paper cover. For example, a book that features modes of transportation might be titled "Go, Go, Go."

4. Have the child glue a sticker (or other picture) on each interior page, placing it on the far right of the page. Using a predictable text pattern, write a sentence on each page that tells about the sticker. In keeping with the transportation theme,

Materials

* construction paper (12 by 18 inches, one sheet)

* manila paper (12 by 18 inches; two sheets)

* stickers (packages with a theme, such as farm animals, work well) or picture cards

* library pocket (optional)

* sentence strip (optional)

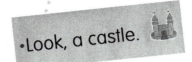
•Look, a castle.

the sentences in a book might read "The car can go. The train can go. The plane can go. The bus can go." Other sample predictable patterns include:

- [Child's name] is my friend.
- I see a [name an object].
- Look, a [name an object].
- I like [name a favorite person or thing].
- [Child's name] can see a [name an object].
- [Child's name] can see [name a person].

5. For additional support, you might write the first letter of the word that names the picture in a different color. Place a green dot at the beginning of each sentence (see sample, left) to indicate where to begin reading.

Teaching With the Books

1. Introduce the books by first arranging five to ten small objects (such as different-color Unifix cubes) in a row in front of the child. Invite the child to "read the row," beginning with the object on the left. Have the child point to each object in turn and name it (for example, by color). Explain that reading is like this: You look at and read each word from left to right.

2. Look at the book cover and read the title with the child. Model reading behaviors, pointing to each word as you move from left to right across the page. Let the child try the same thing.

3. Continue in this way to read each page, pointing to the green dot to show where you begin reading. Revisit the pages to notice the beginning and end of a sentence, spaces between words, familiar words, words that match the picture, and so on.

Back-Cover Pocket Activity

A back-cover pocket activity holds word cards children can match up to a sentence in the book.

1. Glue a library pocket to the back cover of the book. Write a sentence from the book on a sentence strip. Cut apart the sentence word by word. Place the word cards inside the pocket.

2. When the child is finished reading the book, invite him or her to remove the word cards. Have the child find the words that look the same, then reassemble the sentence, placing each word card beneath the matching word. Encourage children to use clues on the cards for help. For example, they may notice that one word begins with a capital letter and one has punctuation after it, both of which provide clues about placement in the sentence.

3. Reread the sentence together. Ask: "Does it sound right? Does it make sense?"

Variations

✳ **Rebus Book:** Use a predictable text pattern, along with stickers or other pictures, to make a rebus-format book. (See sample, right.) Let the child choose several themed stickers, such as a cake, a gift box, a party hat, and balloons for a "birthday" book. Write the text on each page, having the child place the sticker in the sentence in place of the word (or use both the word and the picture).

•I see a ⬜ .

✳ **Themed Books:** Create long books to reinforce vocabulary from theme units. For a unit on polar animals, for example, the predictable text might read "This is a penguin." Let the child name a polar animal to complete the sentence on each page. Provide a matching picture for each animal. For a unit on healthy eating habits, the predictable text might read "I like apples." Let the child name different healthy foods he or she likes and use them to complete the sentence on each page. Provide a picture of each food.

✳ **My Family Books:** Create long books about children's families, featuring a different person on each page. Use a predictable text pattern to name each person (or pet): "This is my [mother, father, sister, brother, pet, etc.]." Illustrate each page with a photograph or the child's drawing of that family member.

Literature Links

While these books do not have a long book format, they do feature predictable text and other details that support print awareness.

I Went Walking by Sue Williams (Harcourt, 1992): "I went walking / What did I see? / I saw a black cat / Looking at me." The cat follows the boy in this story, as does a cast of other animal characters, including a brown horse, a red cow, a green duck, a pink pig, and a yellow dog. The rhyming, predictable text pattern makes this a rewarding book for young children to read.

My Five Senses by Aliki (Crowell, 1989): In this exploration of the five senses, repetitive text and a strong picture-word match reinforce helpful reading behaviors.

Thump, Thump, Rat-a-Tat-Tat by Gene Baer (HarperCollins, 1989): Readers join up with a marching band that parades across the pages. Repetitive text invites children to chime in and inventive use of type reinforces concepts about print, including the understanding that letters come in different shapes and sizes.

Cut-Up Sentence Books

These books give children a wonderful opportunity to assemble sentences. This puzzle-like approach also provides teachers with a window into a child's thinking—and serves as a powerful way to establish and secure the early behaviors of reading.

Materials

- construction paper (one 12- by 18-inch sheet)
- colored tagboard (one 12- by 18-inch sheet)
- white tagboard (1- by 12-inch strips)
- stickers (or other pictures)
- library pocket (optional)
- sentence strip (optional)

Reading Skills Support

✳ Assembling cut-up sentences word by word, leaving a small space between each word, reinforces the reason for those spaces, by helping children understand that print corresponds word-for-word to speech.

✳ The actual hands-on placement of the word cards on the page reinforces left-to-right directionality.

✳ The puzzle-like approach adds a playful element, keeping motivation high.

How to Make the Books

1. Fold the construction paper in half length-wise. (This becomes the front and back cover.)

2. Fold the colored tagboard in half the same way. Place the colored tagboard inside the construction paper and staple at the fold to bind. Note that you can substitute other types of paper when making these books, but it is important to use white (or light) paper for the sentence strips (see step 4) and darker paper for the book pages. This creates contrast between the words and page (background) and highlights the spaces between the words to help children visually make sense of the text.

3. Choose a topic and title for the book based on a conversation with the child—for example, about a family pet. Write a title on the cover (for example, "My Cat, Mo") and invite the child to illustrate it (or use a photo).

4. Write sentences based on your conversation on the tagboard strips—for example, "Mo is my cat." With the child, cut apart each sentence by phrases or word by word, saying each word slowly as you cut. Cut apart the end punctuation as well.

5. With the child, assemble each sentence on a page in the book. Be sure to leave a space between each word and a small space between the last word and the end punctuation. As you do so, talk with the child about placement (spacing) and left-to-right directionality.

6. Read each sentence together after assembling, and glue in place on the book pages (leaving a space between each word).

Teaching With the Books

1. Read each sentence together. Model reading behaviors—for example, point to each word in turn and note the end punctuation. (Discuss any question marks or exclamation points that may have been used, and how they change the sound of a sentence.)

2. As you read, discuss placement, left-to-right directionality, and punctuation with the child. You might say: "This is where we start. This is the way we go. This is where we go after that. And this is where the sentence ends."

3. Take another opportunity, as you read, to point out and discuss the spaces between words, demonstrating for the child that print corresponds to speech.

4. Finally, read through the book again. The child may read aloud independently (if he or she is able) or together with you. As you read each sentence, have the child point to each word in turn, reinforcing awareness of directionality and word-speech correspondence.

Teaching Tip

You might at first cut apart the sentences by phrases, following natural breaks in the language. Progress to cutting apart sentences word-by-word as the child is able. When the child is ready, encourage independent construction of the cut-up sentences. Notice how the child works, and look for evidence of print awareness (for example, that words are organized from left to right on the page).

Back-Cover Pocket Activity

Extend the learning with a back-cover pocket activity that reveals a special message.

1. Glue a library pocket to the back cover.

2. On a sentence strip, write a special message to the child (using known words). Cut apart the message word by word (and end punctuation, too). Place the cards in the pocket along with a sticker that relates to the sentence.

3. Have the child take out the materials and assemble the cards to build a sentence.

✳ **Mini Cut-Up Sentence Books:** Make a smaller cut-up sentence book featuring simple patterned text. Provide pictures that closely match the text.

✳ **Class Big Book of Cut-Up Sentences:** To support an area of study, let each child help create a page for a Big Book of Cut-Up Sentences. Have children write (or copy) their sentences on sentence strips. Guide them to notice where each word begins and ends, and to cut the sentence apart in those places. Each child can then put the sentence back together on a sheet of paper, glue it in place, and illustrate it.

✳ **Pocket Sentence Books:** Glue library pockets (or envelopes) to each left page of a spread. Write sentences on strips of white paper and cut them apart word by word (or by phrases). Place each set of cards in the corresponding pocket. Use stickers or draw pictures to illustrate the right-facing page of each spread (to match the sentence), leaving space at the bottom for children to assemble the sentence. To read the book, children take out the word cards on each page and arrange them in order on the picture page, reading them as they go.

Literature Links

Share books that offer support for early reading behaviors, such as those with simple text and layout and a good match between text and pictures. Books from guided reading collections at the emergent and early levels are a good resource. Following are several examples; or choose other books with similar features.

Cat on the Mat by Brian Wildsmith (HarperCollins, 1986): "The cat sat on the mat." With simple text and supportive illustrations on each page, the books in the Cat on the Mat series support young readers in developing early reading behaviors.

Dressing-up by Jenny Giles, Beverley Randell, and Annette Smith (Rigby, 1996): "I am a rabbit. I am a cat." Children dress up in this story, which features patterned text, strong picture support, and a consistent print layout, helping the reader to establish and secure the early behaviors of reading.

Plop! by June Melser (Wright Group, 1990): "I can see the fish." A little frog shares what he sees in the pond. Simple, predictable text and consistent print layout support emergent readers as they take on the early behaviors of reading.

Layer Books

With their unusual layered pages, these books are fun to make and read. Children are drawn to these books to see what lies beneath each of the special pages, and once they discover how easy it is to make them, they will be eager to try the format on their own. The sample, right, is based on *Rain*, adapted by Rozanne Lanczak Williams (Creative Teaching Press, 1998).

Materials

♦ copy paper
♦ stickers (or other pictures)

Reading Skills Support

❋ With predictable text patterns, layer books create a visual repetition of words, building word recognition.

❋ Layer books naturally draw children's eyes to the picture when they lift each page, reinforcing the connection between pictures and text.

How to Make the Books

1. Stack several sheets of paper together and stagger them as shown (right). Holding the paper securely, fold the top down to meet the bottom edge. Crease at the fold and staple to bind.

2. Choose a topic and write the title on the top page. Select an appropriate text pattern and write a sentence on each additional page (on the strip that extends from each sheet).

3. Add simple illustrations to each page that support the text (placed so the illustration is revealed when the child lifts the page).

Teaching With the Books

1. Read the title together. Let the child point out known letters or words.

2. Notice the sentences on each page. Look at words that are the same and different. (See Teaching Tip, left.)

3. Read the pages together, lifting each page to reveal the illustrations. Guide the child in checking the picture for clues about unknown words in the sentence.

Back-Cover Pocket Activity

Letter cards let children practice spelling and reading story words.

1. Glue a library pocket to the back of the book.

2. Inside the pocket, place letter cards that spell a word from the story.

3. After reading the book, have children arrange the cards to spell the word (revisiting the story for help if needed and to check their spelling). Have children read the word they make.

Variations

✳ **Birthday Cake Layer Books:** Turn a layer book into a birthday treat for a child's special day. Use a marker to outline the outer edge of the book. Add construction-paper candles to the top. Write a "birthday" sentence on each layer and draw a picture or place a sticker to be revealed when the child lifts each layer.

✳ **Poetry Layer Books:** Choose a simple poem, and use it to create a book, writing each line of the poem on a separate layer, and adding a supporting illustration.

Literature Links

Look for books that invite layer book innovations.

The Grouchy Ladybug by Eric Carle (HarperCollins, 1999): The day's events are sequenced through a series of layered pages, as a grouchy ladybug looks for "somebody bigger" to fight.

The Very Hungry Caterpillar by Eric Carle (Penguin, 1986): This layered book sequences the events of the story day by day as a hungry caterpillar looks for food.

The setup of these books is such that children's eyes will naturally be drawn to the text. (Each sentence is visible, but the illustrations are hidden from view.) Let children read the words they see repeated—for example, in the sample "Rain," the words *Rain*, *Rain*, *Rain* (as well as *on* and *the*). Notice words that don't follow that pattern (*rooftop*, *trees*, *me*).

Bubble Books

Speech bubble books are fun to make and read. With text that represents a child's natural language, these books help readers understand that what they say can be written, and that words correspond to speech, word for word. The books also create meaningful opportunities to establish for the child the relationship that exists between reading and writing.

Reading Skills Support

❋ Speech bubbles reinforce the understanding that text corresponds to speech.

❋ Children who enjoy comic books will easily make the connection to speech bubbles in other books.

❋ The use of speech bubbles offers an out-of-the ordinary reading experience, and is a motivating feature for many children.

How to Make the Books

1. Make multiple copies of the speech bubble templates. Cut them out and set them aside.

2. A good starting place for making these books is a book about people who are important to the child. Introduce the book by saying, "Today we are going to make a book about the people you love. Tell me the names of the people who are important to you." As you discuss the topic, have the child draw a picture of himself or herself. (You might draw one of yourself, too, so the child can see an example.)

3. While the child draws, and the two of you talk, record in speech bubbles the child's words, using a predictable text pattern if appropriate (for example, "I love my mom."). As you write, model left-to-right directionality and spacing between words. Share the pen and let the child write known letters and words.

Materials

- ◆ speech bubble templates (page 76)
- ◆ tagboard (9- by 12-inch sheets)
- ◆ construction paper (12- by 18-inch sheet)
- ◆ library pocket (optional)
- ◆ sticky dots (optional)

4. Make photocopies of the child's drawing (one for each speech bubble). Then, with the child, glue the pictures and speech bubbles to the tagboard book pages. Fold the construction paper in half to create the front and back cover. Place the pages inside and staple to bind. Write the title inside a speech bubble, glue it to the cover, and either glue another copy of the child's picture on the cover or have the child draw a new one.

To build fluency skills, remind children that when people speak, they often use expression in their voice. Share some examples from the day's conversations. When children read their bubble books, they can use expression to match the content of the speech bubble. For example, a child reading the speech bubble "I love ice cream" might naturally read with enthusiasm and place emphasis on the word *love*.

Teaching With the Books

1. Preview the book with the child, explaining that speech bubbles are a way to show what someone is saying or thinking. Make a connection between the child's picture on each page and the speech bubble: These are his or her own words.

2. Read the book together, beginning with the cover and pointing to each word.

3. As you read, guide the child to notice how the words in each speech bubble match what the child said. Encourage the child to look for known words and read with natural expression.

Back-Cover Pocket Activity

A back-cover library pocket holds quotation marks for placing around the child's words on each page, providing a lesson in the punctuation that is sometimes used with speech bubbles.

1. Glue a library pocket to the back cover of the book.

2. Make a set of sticky-dot quotation marks for each speech bubble in the book (leave the backing on the dots). Use a different-color marker for each set (or use different-color sticky dots). Place the quotation marks in the pocket.

3. When the child is finished reading the book, invite him or her to remove the contents of the pocket. Explain that sometimes the words in a speech bubble are placed inside quotation marks—one at the beginning and one at the end. When readers see quotation marks, it is a sign that someone is "speaking." Let the child pair up the quotation marks by color, then place them around each sentence. Encourage the child to notice and share with you quotation marks used in other books.

Variations

✳ **More Bubble Books:** Speech bubbles can have different shapes—balloons, boxes, circles, even clouds. (See samples, right.) Let children experiment with using different-shaped speech bubbles. Explain that the cloud shape is often used to show what someone is thinking, but not saying.

✳ **Comic-Strip-Style Books:** Create an oversized comic-strip template for children to use with speech bubbles. Divide a large horizontal sheet of paper into several segments. Have children draw pictures to show a sequence of events. Provide speech bubbles for them to glue on the comic strip. Let them dictate words as necessary.

✳ **Sticky-Note Speech Bubble Books:** Turn a wordless picture book into a speech bubble book. Choose a children's book with few or no words, such as the mesmerizing *Good Night, Gorilla* by Peggy Rathbun (Putnam, 1996). Let children suggest what characters in the pictures might be saying or thinking. Write children's words on large sticky notes and outline with speech bubbles. Place on the corresponding pages, then read the book.

Literature Links

After children have read their own speech bubble books, have more fun with this text feature by sharing these books.

Knuffle Bunny, A Cautionary Tale by Mo Willems (Hyperion, 2004): "Where's Knuffle Bunny?" The speech bubbles in this book express the emotions of Trixie and her mom after discovering that Knuffle Bunny, a favorite stuffed animal, is missing. After reading this book write a class bubble book about feelings.

Millions to Measure by David M. Schwartz (HarperCollins, 2003): As Marvelosissimo the Mathematical Magician explains the history of measurement, speech bubbles let other characters in this comical book share comments and questions.

Tall by Jez Alborough (Walker Books, 2005): Dissatisfied with feeling small, Bobo the chimp makes his way through the jungle, climbing on a succession of increasingly larger animals until he takes a tumble from the kangaroo's head. Simple text is set in speech bubbles, encouraging the connection between speech and print.

Easy-to-Make Books That Target Specific Reading Needs © 2009 by Florence Miyamoto and Joan Novelli, Scholastic Teaching Resources

Theme-Based Easy-to-Make Books

Following are suggestions for creating more easy-to-make books that will capture children's attention, teach essential skills, and support reading success.

Birthday Books

These special books make a wonderful treat on a child's birthday, or whenever a child just wants to write and read about birthdays.

1. Make copies of the cake template (page 80). Glue each cake template to tagboard and trim to size.

2. Invite the child to fill in the sentence at the top of each page: "I like _____ cake." (To substitute a different text pattern, place a strip of white paper over the sentence, and write in a new sentence, then photocopy.) Children can fill in the blank with a cake flavor, such as *vanilla*, *chocolate*, or *applesauce*. Or, they can fill in the blanks with color words, such as *yellow*, *pink*, and *orange*.

3. Place cake pages in between a construction paper cover and staple to bind. Decorate the cover like a birthday cake, complete with candles.

4. Extend the Birthday Book by having the child bring in photographs of past birthday parties. Write a caption for each photo. Glue the photos and captions (one set per page) to sheets of construction paper and put them together to make a personal Book of Birthdays for the child.

Teaching Tip

Share another birthday book. *Happy Birthday, Moon,* by Frank Asch (Simon & Schuster, 1982), is a charming story about a little bear who is looking for the perfect birthday gift for the moon. After reading, ask the child about a favorite birthday party, a yummy cake, the best present, or other special memories.

Color Books

What is red? What is green? Color words are among those included in the Dolch Basic Sight Vocabulary 220 list. Make books that provide repeated practice with these words, one for each color.

1. Share *Mouse Paint* by Ellen Stoll Walsh (Harcourt, 1989), the delightful story of three white mice who find three jars of paint. After reading, generate a list of the color words the mice discover.

2. Let the child choose a color word from the list. Staple sheets of tagboard (or construction paper) together to make a book. Using a marker in that target color, write the color word on the cover as the title—for example, "Green." To support left-to-right directionality, place a dot in the same color at the beginning of the word.

3. Invite the child to name things that are that color. Gather pictures (use stickers, cut pictures from magazines or old workbooks, or use the child's drawings), and glue one on each page. Color the pictures to match the color word if necessary.

4. Choose a predictable text pattern to use on each page and write a sentence that names the object and color—for example, "A fire truck is red." Use a marker in that color to write the first letter of the color word.

Teaching Tip

Create a class cookie book. Give each child a cookie-shaped sheet of tagboard. Have children decorate their cookie, then dictate (or write) a sentence about it. Put the pages together to make a class "Big Cookie Book."

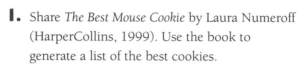

Cookie Books

As a subject for books, cookies is always a high-interest choice.

1. Share *The Best Mouse Cookie* by Laura Numeroff (HarperCollins, 1999). Use the book to generate a list of the best cookies.

2. Staple five sheets of tagboard together to make a blank book. Cut out a construction-paper oval (cookie) that is just a little smaller than the size of the book, and glue to the cover. Write the title inside the oval. Cut out smaller brown construction paper circles (more cookies), "decorate" with "chocolate chip" dots or colored-paper "sprinkles," and add the cookies to the cover.

3. With the child, choose cookie words from the list. Provide an appropriate sentence pattern for the child to complete (such as "I like _____ cookies."). Write the child's sentence across the bottom of each page.

4. Provide cookie shapes the child can decorate and glue to each page.

Garden Books

Planting seeds, waiting for spring, watching flowers grow . . . gardens are a source of inspiration for making books.

1. Share Lois Ehlert's *Planting a Rainbow* (Harcourt, 1998), a colorful look at planning, planting, and picking flowers in a garden.

2. Use the story as a springboard to make books with children. Fold sheets of 12-by 18-inch tagboard, and place them in between a sheet of folded construction paper (the same size). Staple to bind. Write the title on the cover—for example, "Bianca's Garden."

3. Provide simple construction-paper shapes and let the child put them together to create a different-color flower on each page (or provide stickers), and a "garden" of flowers (one of each color on the previous pages) on the last page.

4. Choose an appropriate sentence pattern and use it to write about the flower on each page—for example, "Here is a red flower." Vary the sentence pattern slightly on the last page: "Here is Bianca's garden." To reinforce concepts about print, stretch each sentence across the page, exaggerating the space between each word.

Content-Area Books

Design books to support any content area theme, such as a science unit on oceans or the human body. (See page 15 for a list of themes.)

1. Choose a topic, such as "oceans." Decide on an appropriate sentence pattern—for example, "I can see a [name of ocean creature]." Brainstorm with children words to complete each page.

2. Make a basic book, placing tagboard sheets in between colored construction-paper covers and stapling to bind. Add creative details to the pages for visual appeal—for example, a book about oceans might have a "wave" of blue paper across the bottom half to represent water.

3. Write a sentence across the top portion of each page. Let children add illustrations—for example, gluing a sea-creature picture they've drawn (or placing a sticker) in the "water" on each page of an ocean book.

4. Add special finishing touches to each page; for instance, bits of glitter will make fish in an ocean book sparkle in the water.

5. As an extension, glue a library pocket to the back cover. Make a word card for each "picture" word from the story. (These are words that name items that are easily pictured.) For an "ocean" book, these words might include *seahorse*, *fish*, *crab*, and *turtle*. Place a picture (such as a sticker) that goes with each word on an index card and trim to fit in the library pocket. Children can take out the word and picture cards and match them up for further word recognition practice.

I like _____ cake.